# MY DOG'S GOT NO NOSE

# MY DOG'S GOT NO NOSE

by Ron Aldridge

## JOSEF WEINBERGER PLAYS

LONDON

MY DOG'S GOT NO NOSE
First published in 2011
by Josef Weinberger Ltd
12-14 Mortimer Street, London, W1T 3JJ
www.josef-weinberger.com
general.info@jwmail.co.uk

ISBN    978 0 85676 303 8

Printed in England by Good News Digital Books, Ongar, Essex

MY DOG'S GOT NO NOSE was first presented by Bruce James Productions Ltd at the Key Theatre Studio, Peterborough on 29th October 2009 prior to a UK tour. The cast was as follows:

THE MAN                    Damian Williams

Directed by Bruce James
Set and Lighting Designed by Geoff Gilder
Costume Designs by Bruce James

## ACT ONE

THE MAN, *in his 50s, is sitting at a table in a sparsely furnished small room. There is a single bed and beside the bed is a small chest of drawers, on which are some folded clothes, with a towel draped over them.*

*On the table is a large, opened wooden box. It is a 'make-up' box, and inside the lid is a small mirror. There are lights around the mirror, and the room has the feel of a rather 'seedy' dressing room.*

*There are three or four hats on the table above the make-up box and a jacket is hanging on the back of the chair.*

*He wears a dressing gown and is looking into the mirror, applying a touch of stage make-up.*

*He continues looking into the mirror, and starts to rehearse.*

THE MAN       Before I became a comedian I used to be . . . no . . . before I became a stand-up comic I used to be . . . no . . . before I became a stand-up comedian I used to be a furniture salesman.

              (*He gradually turns, gets up and addresses the audience.*)

              I used to travel all over the world, exhibitions and things. I remember I was at a furniture show in Budapest, and after the show one evening I went to a little bar round the corner. I was having a drink, and I noticed that on the next table to me was this beautiful girl. I was looking at her, and she was looking at me. We smiled, and then she beckoned for me to come and join her. Which I did. But then I was stuck.

              I couldn't speak Hungarian, and she couldn't speak English. But we got by. I drew little pictures on the napkin.

I drew a bottle with bubbles coming out of the top, showed it to her, she nodded, and we had a bottle of champagne.

I drew a chicken, showed it to her, she nodded, and we had chicken to eat.

I then drew a cup and saucer, showed it to her, she nodded, and we had a cup of coffee. So, the evening went fine, and as we were about to leave, she took the napkin from me . . . and she drew a bed on it.

Yes. I know. Isn't that amazing?

But what I couldn't understand was . . . how did she know I was a furniture salesman?

The thing about stand-up comedy, is that you've got to get your audience with your first joke. So that one should do, shouldn't it? What do you think? You sure now, it's very important. Okay, I'll do it.

You see, tonight I am realising a dream. A dream that's been close to my heart for over thirty years.

In . . . (*He looks at his watch.*) . . . about three quarters of an hour or so, I shall walk through that door . . . (*He indicates to the left side of the stage.*) . . . into what is affectionately termed in the business as 'the lion's den', and I will make my debut as a stand-up comedian.

Over thirty years I've waited for this, can't believe it's actually going to happen. No turning back now though, the audience will be starting to turn up.

It's the toughest you know, stand-up comedy. That's what they say. It's been the death of many a good man that's for sure.

Just wish I wasn't so nervous. I've been to the toilet four times, re-done my make-up three times, and thrown-up twice. And this is for something I really want to do!

They say it's part of the process, being nervous. 'It's good for you', they say. I'm not so sure.

I was told once that people don't actually get nervous. They think they do, but they don't. What happens is, that when you think about the difficult task ahead, the body sends a message to the brain . . . fear, doubt, worry, anxiety, concern, danger. The brain then produces a chemical to help the body cope with that fear. The chemical it produces is called adrenaline. And what this chemical, this drug does . . . because it is a drug . . . what this drug does is to make you highly-alert, highly-focused, and highly-concentrated. No matter what is happening in your life, all you think about is the task ahead.

You see, the adrenaline converts into energy, either physically or mentally, to help you cope. If you wake up in the middle of the night for example, because you think you've heard a noise, you get a rush of adrenaline, and you strain to listen. You can almost hear better. Once you realise there's no problem, you relax, the adrenaline subsides, and you get back to normal. You could be chased by a bull in a field and there's a high fence. You'll get over that fence . . . and the next day you'll look and think . . . 'how the hell did I get over that?'

It's the adrenaline converting into energy. It's instant.

In this case however, it's different. When I think about . . . (*He looks at his watch.*) . . . what's about to happen, it's not instant. The drug is produced and is in my body, but it won't help me until I start. So while I'm waiting, I have this excess of unused chemical in my body.

Now, an excess of different chemicals in the body
has a variety of different reactions. An excess of
adrenaline in the body causes feelings of unease,
discomfort . . . slight nausea even. You could be
physically shaking, your palms could be sweating
. . . and all these feelings are what we call nerves.
But actually, you're not nervous at all . . . the fact
is, you are just temporarily chemically imbalanced!

So, I'm not going to be nervous any more . . . (*He
starts to pace around the room.*) . . . chemical
reaction, chemical reaction, chemical reaction!

(*He stops and looks at his watch again.*)

I've been ready for ages. Oh . . . what do you think
of the costume by the way?

(*He takes off his dressing gown to reveal a very
'colourful and loud' costume – maybe striped or
checked trousers that are possibly a little short
for him, with very colourful socks and some big
boots. The shirt has a very colourful and over-
the-top design, with possibly a sparkly
waistcoat.*)

Look all right does it? I don't know whether to
wear the jacket or not.

(*He crosses back, gets the jacket that is hanging
on the back of the chair and puts it on. Again,
this could be a rather outrageous design.*)

What do you think? With or without the jacket?

(*He tries to get suggestions from some of the
audience.*)

Oh, hang on . . . there's a choice of hats too.

(*He crosses back to the table to the hats.*)

A lot of comedians use hats. There's this one . . .

(*He tries the first one on, a comedy-type bobble hat, and then strikes a pose.*)

. . . or this one . . .

(*He swaps to another one, a winter hat with ear flaps, and poses again.*)

What do you think? The first, or this one?

(*Again he looks for suggestions from some of the audience. He then picks up the third one, a trilby 'spiv' type.*)

What about this one? This is good. You see, comedians can do funny 'business' with hats . . . it can almost fall off . . . (*He does a drunken stagger and holds the hat on.*) . . . you can throw it to the ground in either disgust or anger . . . (*He throws the hat to the ground.*) "I will not go there!" Something like that . . . depending on the joke.

(*He picks up the hat.*)

This is good . . .

(*He tries rolling the hat down his arm.*)

. . . if you can do it of course.

(*He looks at the hats.*)

Mmm . . . can't make my mind up.

(*There is an opportunity here for the actor to do an impersonation with the fourth hat if he wishes – a Tommy Cooper fez, for example.*)

You see . . . I didn't want to be too 'flash'. I wanted the right sort of balance between a sophisticated entertainer and a total pillock. I think I've got it, don't you?

(*He crosses back up, puts the hats back on the
table, takes off the jacket, hangs it on the back of
the chair and then sits.*)

My wife, Judith, thinks I'm crazy you know . . . she
always has done. She can't understand it. Not
sure I can actually . . . it's just something I've
always wanted to do. I suppose everyone's got
something they've always wanted to do . . . or be.

But why do I want to do this? It's not as though
it's easy . . . I mean, you can't get away with
anything can you? In most jobs you can get away
with things, can't you? You can make a mistake,
and it's not disastrous . . . you can pretend to be
working . . . you can 'skive' off early . . . you can
get away with things. But if I tell a joke and no
one laughs . . . well that's it isn't it? Bloody
nightmare.

I don't know, maybe it's the danger . . . the risk.
We all like a bit of danger now and again don't
we? (*He looks at the audience.*) Don't we?

It's just that it's . . . well it's just so wonderful to
hear people laugh. I love making people laugh.
And I've got better at it as I've got older. I was
never funny when I was young. Which was a pity,
because I think it would have helped with the
girls.

Well that's what they say . . . get a girl laughing
and you're half-way there. Is that right girls? (*He
looks at some ladies in the audience.*) Is it?

(*He rises.*)

Because I had trouble with girls when I was
younger you know. I know it's difficult for you to
believe that as you sit there and gaze at the
Adonis before you, but I did. I was hopeless. You
see, in my day the man was always supposed to
take the initiative. Not like now. Girls are quite

brazen these days. I wish they'd been brazen in my day. Would have made my life much easier. In my day they just sent out 'discreet signs' . . . but of course I was such an idiot I didn't see these signs. I was getting nowhere. And when I did get somewhere . . . I was too polite! When a girl said no, I thought she meant no.

All my mates were saying . . .
"Of course she didn't mean no."
"But she said no."
"Yeah but it depends on the no. Some no's could be a 'maybe', some could be a 'keep trying' . . . some could even be a yes."
It was all very confusing . . . for an idiot like me.

And the confusion always seemed to be at its worst when I finally managed to get my hand on the inner thigh.

Ah, the inner thigh. Oh how I love the inner thigh.

Some men go for boobs, some for bums, some for legs . . . but for me, it's the inner thigh.
It's a very neglected part of the female anatomy. It's so soft and wonderful and . . . let's not go there right now. But when your hand is there . . . on the inner thigh . . . (*He sits on the end of the bed and demonstrates.*) . . . the level of expectation and anticipation is at its greatest. Anything could happen. The slightest movement . . . and we all know where we stand.

I used to like leaving my hand there for a few seconds . . . not moving . . . to heighten the tension . . . and then I'd just 'twitch' my fingers . . . knowing that . . . if there was going to be a no, that's where the no was going to come. And . . . whatever type of no it was, whether she just said no, or if she slapped my hand . . . I just stopped. So near yet so far. I was getting nowhere, and it was driving me crazy.

I blame my mother. I do.

(*He rises.*)

I was never given the 'facts of life' as such. When
I was a teenager I was just given two bits of
advice. "Now that you've started taking girls
out," she said, "remember these two things. One:
Always act like a gentleman, and Two: never
punch girls in the stomach."

And that was it. My facts of life. "Well mother,
I'd never actually thought about that, but fair
enough." No wonder I was a slow starter. But the
advice must have worked, because I can honestly
say, that up till now, I have always tried to act like
a gentleman, and I have never ever punched a girl
in the stomach.

And then I met Judith. My wife.

We were at a dance . . . there was always a local
dance on a Saturday night. You know the sort of
thing . . . girls on one side dancing round their
handbags . . . blokes on the other side getting
pissed. They were getting pissed so they could
pluck up the courage to ask a girl for a dance. I
wasn't a brilliant dancer I have to admit . . .
although I was good at the 'twist'.

(*He starts to do the 'Twist' – not very well, and
rather 'comedic'. NB: it could be a different
dance if the actor prefers.*)

Well . . . I thought so anyway. At least it made
people laugh.

Anyway, after a few drinks I was trying my luck
. . . and getting lots of "no thank you's" . . . I was
getting nowhere. And then I spotted Judith. She
wasn't the most beautiful bloom in the bouquet . . .
but she wasn't the worst.

"She'll do." I thought. "Well . . . worth a try
anyway."

It was getting near the end of the evening . . . and they always have a couple of slow songs at the end . . .

"Won't be able to impress her with my 'twist,' I thought, "but never mind, it's too late in the evening to worry about that now."

I walked across . . . (*He 'cooly' moves across.*) . . . trying to look really 'cool' because I'd seen she'd spotted me . . . (*He stops and looks at the audience.*) . . . excuse me, I can be 'cool' you know . . . and I asked her for a dance.

Amazingly, she said yes.

We had a couple of slow 'smooches' . . . she didn't seem to worry that I trod on her toes five times . . . and after that, we started dating.

I didn't think she was my type actually . . . I don't even know why we kept going out together. Of course it may have had something to do with the fact that she was the first girl who didn't say no.

Can you imagine? I couldn't believe my luck.

"Are you sure?" I said. "Oh get on with it." she said.

And that was that. True lust. Next thing you know we're married. It was all so . . . quick. Bit too bloody quick really.

That's the trouble you see . . . sometimes we rush into these things . . . we don't really think about it enough.

(*He crosses back, sits at the table and checks his make-up.*)

They say that you're ruled by either your heart or your head. But young blokes are ruled by neither of those.

At that age it's the 'willy' that rules. You just
seem to follow where your 'willy' takes you. I
suppose that's how it happened with me and
Judith . . . I just agreed to everything.

"I think we should get married." "Yes dear."

"I think you should propose." "Yes dear."

"I think it should be soon." "Yes dear."

You're not thinking you see . . . you're not really
listening . . . you're just wondering when you'll
next get to visit the inner thigh. The 'willy' rules!

I remember getting ready on the morning of my
wedding thinking . . .

"How the hell did this happen?" By then of course
it's too bloody late.

Any of you blokes here recognise that feeling?

(*He looks at them.*)

What am I saying? Hardly likely to admit it if
you've got your wife sitting beside you are you?
Bet there's one of two of you though. In fact, I'm
bloody sure of it.

I could have just run away of course . . . but that's
not easy either. Anyone here tried that? (*He
stops.*) Sorry chaps . . . shouldn't keep asking
should I?

And so I got married.

(*He stops and looks at his watch.*)

How are we doing for time? Oh God . . . (*He gets
up and starts pacing.*) . . . chemical reaction,
chemical reaction, chemical reaction!

(*He stops.*)

What if they don't laugh?  Oh my God!  Big
chemical reaction!

(*He paces again, then stops.*)

Of course they'll laugh . . . of course they will.

(*He crosses back and looks in the mirror.*)

Make-up look all right?

(*He calms himself, moves across, sits on the end of
the bed and re-ties his shoelaces.  There was
nothing wrong with them, he's just dealing with
the nerves.*)

Anyway . . . shortly after we married I started my
own business.  Photographer.  That was my
profession . . . well, until now.  Did very well, quite
successful really.  Did anything to start with . . .
weddings, portraits . . . anything.  Then the work
got better, and I did a lot of adverts in those
glossy magazines.  It was good stuff.

Never got the girls in their underwear though, or
bikinis.  Shame really, I'd have liked that.  That
sort of work never seemed to come my way.  I
usually got the chunk of cheddar on a table in a
country kitchen.  Or hosepipes.  Tell me, how can
you possibly make hosepipes interesting?

So, there I was, successful photographer with all
the trappings . . . nice big house, two cars etc, etc
. . . and all I really wanted to be was a stand-up
comedian.

So that was the problem really.  She could see this
very comfortable life-style of ours being
threatened by these stupid ideas of mine.  You
know what she said to me one day?

"You . . . a stand-up comedian?  Don't be so
ridiculous.  Everyone'll laugh at you!"

Thought that was quite nice really.  Not quite
what she meant though.

(*He rises as he looks at his watch again.*)

At times like these you should say to yourself,
now what is the worst that could happen?  The
worst is, I walk through that door, I'm terrible, no
one laughs, and it is totally and unbearably
embarrassing.  They'll laugh about it for a few
days, I'll take a week to get over it, and then it's
all back to normal.

Now is that so terrible?  Oh my God . . . (*He paces
again.*) . . . chemical reaction, chemical reaction,
chemical reaction!

(*He crosses back up, and again looks in the
mirror.*)

Make-up look all right?

(*He calms himself, sits in front of the mirror and
makes some make-up adjustments.*)

Judith had her dream too. She wanted to move out,
buy a big place in the country, and breed dogs.
Dog-lover she is.

I was always able to postpone that terrifying
possibility, saying I was not prepared to sell my
business.  I told her I wouldn't get such good
photographic work if I was outside the city.
That's what I convinced her of anyway.

And I loved the buzz of the city . . . always
something happening.  I could go and see
comedians working anytime I wanted. Watch them,
study them . . . pinch stuff from them . . . it was
brilliant.  I felt I was at the heart of it all.

The drawback of course, was that, if I wasn't
prepared to give up my photographic business for

her dream, then I couldn't really give it up for mine, could I?

And also, she wasn't all that healthy, Judith. Always been a bit . . . 'frail'. The doctors said she was born with a minor heart defect. The countryside would have been good for her, I'm sure . . . so there was a lot of guilt I had to deal with.

So how come I'm here making my debut?

Well . . . it started because of the dog.

Judith had this dog, King Charles spaniel, pedigree as long as your arm. It's like her child. We don't have children . . . well, we couldn't have children . . . well, she couldn't. We had check-ups . . . I was all right, but she . . .

(*A moment.*)

Shame really, I'd have liked someone calling me dad.

I think it would have made me a better person too . . . being a parent. Wouldn't have been quite so selfish. Would have understood things better maybe, had an appreciation of the miracle of life and all that. But I came to terms with it.

Wasn't too difficult for me, but for Judith it was just terrible. Not easy that for a woman. It's what she's built for. Neither of us wanted to adopt . . . not the same thing is it?

And of course making love becomes a different thing. If you can't ever have children, then it's just about fun. After a few years . . . the 'fun' sort of . . . well . . . just stops.

So it took its toll really, all that. And that's when she got the dog. I mean, I couldn't say no could

I?  And that's where all her love and affection
went.

Not that I've got anything against dogs, it's just
that you have to be careful about people and
animals, don't you?  I don't really mind animals,
but I can take them or leave them, and I've never
really understood this . . . this mania that some
people have.

They say you can always judge a man by the way
he treats animals.  Well I don't agree.  I think
that's a myth put about by animal lovers.  The way
you judge a man is by the way he treats other
people, surely?

And then she goes on about the bullfights in
Spain.  "How terrible, how barbaric.  How could
they treat their animals like that?"  Now, I don't
know what I feel about bullfights, but the fact
remains . . . that country has no need for a Society
for the Prevention of Cruelty to Children.  And
you don't get grannies mugged and raped either.
It's unheard of.

Difficult to question the priorities really.  Mind
you, a society for the poor bulls might not go
amiss.

(*He checks, seems to be satisfied with the make-
up and gets up.*)

Anyway, back to the dog.  The trouble with the
dog is, it's got a pedigree, but it's got no sense.
She never trained it properly or anything, it was
just spoilt.  You couldn't take it off its lead, it
would just run across the street.  If you were in
the park, it would run away and not come back
when you called it.

Crazy animal, no discipline whatsoever.

The road in front of our house is always very
busy, so we had this rule.

The back door was fine because the garden's all
fenced in, but you never, never opened the front
door until you knew where the dog was because it
would just bolt off. So it became a regular thing . . .

"Ah, there's the doorbell . . . where's the dog?"

Now, as I said, this dog hadn't got a lot of sense,
but one thing it did realise was that every time the
doorbell rang we grabbed him, whether he wanted
to be grabbed or not.  So after a while, every time
the doorbell rang, he used to hide.

Can you believe that?  Now we've got to find him,
before we can grab him, before we can open the
door.  I used to get so annoyed.

"Oh this is just ridiculous", and I'd start up the
hall.

"Don't open that door!"

Huge rows we'd have in the hallway with someone
outside listening.  Insane, the whole thing.

Anyway, one day I'm on the phone having a row
with the bank manager, Judith's out somewhere,
and the doorbell goes.

"Ah, there's the doorbell . . . where's the dog?"

I tell the bank manager I'll call him back, and go to
look for the dog.  This time he's well-hidden, can't
find him anywhere.  The doorbell goes again.  'Sod
it' I think . . . and I open the door.

From nowhere, like lightning . . . he's out!

He's done it.  First time in all these years he's
outwitted me.  I start yelling and chasing after him.
Old Mrs Rogers from down the road is at the door
. . . she's come to see Judith . . . she makes a grab

for the dog . . . misses him and nearly ends up in
the flowerbeds!

Off he goes, straight into the  road . . . BANG!
He's hit by a car coming one way . . . bounces off
. . . BANG! Hit by a car coming the other way.

I rush out. Dead. I couldn't believe it. The dog is
dead.

Can you imagine? I mean, this is not just a dog
we're talking about, this is the child! Why
couldn't it have happened when she was here? It
wouldn't have made it any better for the dog, but
it would have made it a bloody sight better for me.

When she did get back, I got the lot.

"It's all your fault! You did it on purpose!
You've always hated the dog! You've always
hated me! You've never loved me! . . . " The lot.
I got the lot.

I won't go into any more detail about the row,
suffice to say that she packed a suitcase and went
to stay with her sister, who lives about ten
minutes away.

Wouldn't see me, wouldn't talk to me, wouldn't
come back . . . that's it, all over. I thought after a
few days it would all calm down and she'd come
back. Three weeks later . . . still nothing. She
would not communicate. And I tried, I really tried.

(*He stops and looks off to the side.*)

Did someone just call me?

(*He crosses to the side and looks off. There is
obviously nobody there. He crosses back.*)

Must be hearing things.

That's the trouble as you get older isn't it?
Everything gets . . . 'inefficient'. It still all works
. . . but only just. Your hearing, your eyesight,
your back, your teeth, your 'willy' . . . your bowel
movements . . . (*He stops and looks at a member
of the audience*.) . . . oh sorry, too much
information was it?

George Burns . . . wonderful American comedian
. . . used to have some lovely material about
getting older. "Bent down to tie my shoelaces the
other day, and wondered what else I could do
while I was down there."

Anyway . . . she was at her sister's place . . . ten
minutes up the road and still wouldn't
communicate.

(*He then suddenly crosses up and looks in the
mirror again.*)

You sure this make-up's all right?

I'm not used to wearing make-up you see. It's the
bloody eye-liner that gets me. Three times I stuck
that stupid stick in my eye trying to get the line
straight. How you girls cope doing that every day
I've no idea. And it is every day isn't it?

"Oooh no, I can't be seen out without my make-
up." Why not? We have to see you at home in all
your glory, why can't others? "Oooh no!" No . . .
I'm glad we don't have to do it every day. Us
blokes are the real thing, what you see is what you
get.

(*A moment.*)

Her sister's lovely. Really lovely. She really is
the best bloom in the bouquet. I've often thought
I married the wrong sister. Actually I don't often
think that, I've always thought that. Sarah her
name is, and she's married to this really boring
pillock called Roger. God he's a bore. Can't

believe she married him. He's no fun, he's always
negative, he's always moaning about something or
other, God knows what she saw in him.

Interesting that isn't it, how couples get together?
You look at some couples and you think, "what
the hell does she see in him?". . . or, "how the hell
did he end up with her?" (*He happens to be
looking at a woman in the audience.*) Oh sorry, I
didn't mean you personally . . .

Interesting though isn't it? Human nature I
suppose. There's no accounting for taste. All to
do with the drive of the 'willy' in one way or
another I should imagine . . . wouldn't you?

(*A moment. He looks at his watch, crosses and sits
on the side of the bed.*)

I remember once, all four of us were invited to this
lunch-party up the street. Judith said she couldn't
go, she was going to some dog show instead . . .
and Roger said he'd go with her as he didn't fancy
going to the party. They were going to be away
till late evening, so I went to the party with Sarah.

Usually I don't drink very much, neither does
Sarah, but we had such a wonderful time together
at this party, that by the time we left we were both
totally pissed. We staggered back to her place,
laughing as we almost fell through the door, and
almost fell on top of each other.

Well, what with the laughter and the drink . . .

(*He stops. A moment.*)

It was just wonderful.

We dozed in each other's arms, and when we
woke, slightly more sober, she was horrified. She
couldn't believe what had happened. She made
me leave immediately, and made me swear to never
talk about it again. 'It was a mistake, it shouldn't

have happened, it'll never happen again, and the best thing is to forget all about it!'

But I couldn't forget it . . . it was wonderful. And it couldn't have been that wonderful if it wasn't 'two-way'. I know she's always liked me.

But she would never discuss it. Never. However hard I tried. And I did try. I tried a lot.

And then of course the years go by, you stop trying . . . but I'll never forget.

(*He stops and pulls himself together.*)

Sorry, where was I? Oh yes, Judith wouldn't come back.

So, I thought, if she's not coming back, then what is there to stop me doing what I really want to do?

(*He stops.*)

Have I got time? (*He looks at his watch.*) I've got time.

(*He rises, very enthusiastic about his subject.*)

Well, it was just . . . wonderful. I got out all my material – the scripts, the films, the DVDs, and I started to seriously work on getting my comedy act together.

It was such a luxury . . . I've never been able to spend so much time on it before. I even took time off work. I pretended to be ill, cancelled appointments, and I just absorbed myself in all this wonderful comedy.

I've got videos and films of all sorts of people . . . those old-time American boys, Bob Hope, Jack Benny, George Burns . . . aah, they made it all look so easy, just standing there. Les Dawson, Ben Elton, Eddie Izzard, Billy Connolly . . . I watched

them all. That way, even if you don't know what
you want to do, you know what you don't want to
do. I tried to develop a style of my own, because I
think I'm better with stories rather than one-liners.
Stories with characters that involve and interest
the audience . . . like my furniture salesman joke.

So I got the whole act together, and wrote little
comedy links between the jokes. I practised and
practised, worked really hard, and I put some
visual stuff in as well, with the legs . . . I've got
good legs, perfect for drunk jokes.

(*He does a drunken stagger.*)

This drunk gets into a taxi.
"Take me to Piccadilly Circus."
The taxi-driver says, "You're in Piccadilly Circus."
"Thanks very much. Next time don't drive so
fast."

(*The 'drunk' staggers off.*)

Good to have a bit of visual humour.

I got together about thirty minutes of material,
rehearsed it up to standard and then thought . . .
what do I do now? I suppose I ought to get a
booking. But how the hell do I do that?

And then the phone call came.

From her sister Sarah. Just finding out if I was all
right, and what was happening.

I told her I was now trying to get a job as a
comedian . . . and two hours later Judith was back
home!

"What's all this about?"
I told her.
"I see." She said. Then came the killer question.

"So, for the first time since we've been married you are prepared to give up your business are you?"

"Er . . . yes."

"Right," she said, "There's always been a choice about what we do if you give up the business. Either we breed dogs in the country or you become a stand-up comedian, is that right?"

"Er . . . yes."

"Well, that choice still exists. So, this is the deal. I will put the house on the market, and you will try and get a job as a comedian. If the house sells before you get the job, we move to the country."

So suddenly, there I am thinking, how the hell did that happen? One minute I'm on my own, happy as Larry . . . the next I'm involved in a race against time.

I kept thinking, this can't be right can it? But of course I had no argument to make. I'd always insisted that I wouldn't give up my business and I wouldn't move away from the city. Now that I'd said I was prepared to give it up . . . that was it. Her dream had to be included too. I hadn't got a leg to stand on.

So now I was really sweating. I know some people can take a year to sell a house, but I also know people who sell within a week.

She was totally confident of course. She thought there's not a man alive who'd employ me as a comic. So she went off to the estate agents, and I set about getting a job. I went to see a theatrical agent.

"Let me see you work."
"But that's why I've come to you . . . for work."

I went to some local clubs.

"What have you done?"
"Well, I'm just starting actually."
"Come back when you've got some experience."
"How can I get experience if you won't give me a chance?"

It was the same everywhere. And it wasn't easy rehearsing my material either, with these terrible people snooping round my house. Sniffy women saying things like, "Well this wallpaper will have to go for a start."

I hate it don't you? I refused to have anything to do with them. Judith used to show them round, making really intelligent remarks like, "This is the bathroom."

What the hell else could it be?

It was a nightmare, and everywhere I went looking for a job the reaction was the same.

Then suddenly, I realised where I was going wrong. It hit me like a thunderbolt out of the blue. Of course I couldn't get a job. Of course no one would employ me. I was being far too honest. It's no good me saying, 'I've got no experience, I'm just starting'. If I'm to have any chance at all, there's only one thing I can do. Lie.

Why not? It's fair enough isn't it? Well, isn't it?

Come on, let's be honest now, there is no such thing as a totally honest person. That animal simply does not exist. Hands up anyone here who thinks they're a totally honest person. A person who doesn't tell lies. Who's never told a lie in their life. Anyone?

(*He looks for a response.*)

Of course there isn't. Everybody is dishonest, some more than others I grant you . . . but that is a fact of life. I mean, life is all about balance. The balance of opposites. Yin and yang, positive and negative, light and dark, honesty and dishonesty, truth and lie. One cannot exist without the other. We kid ourselves by calling them 'little white lies', or we say, 'it's best if she doesn't know the truth', or we tell a lie, 'because we don't want to hurt someone.'

We can call them 'justified' lies, but they're still lies. So the only real truth is . . . that everybody is untruthful. It's right isn't it?

Okay . . . well then, if everybody else is telling lies, why the hell can't I?

So that's what I did. I went round the clubs and I started lying. And you know what happened? That's right, you've guessed it.

We got an offer on the house!

They say that 'timing' is very important in every person's life. Well how about that then? I couldn't believe it.

(*He stops and looks across to the side.*)

Did someone just call me?

(*He goes to the side of the stage and looks off.*)

Oh. Hang on a second.

(*He goes off, and quickly rushes back on.*)

Okay, this is it. Oh God. Chemical reaction, chemical reaction, chemical reaction! Now, you mustn't say good luck, you have to say, 'break a leg'.

(*He looks at the audience.*)

Well go on then . . .

(*He gets them to say it.*)

Thank you.

(*He starts to hurry off, but suddenly stops.*)

Oh, the jacket . . . what do you think? Yes or no?

(*He hurriedly tries to get suggestions.*)

Come on, come on . . . oh for God's sake . . .

(*He rushes over, grabs the jacket and rushes off.*)

Chemical reaction, chemical reaction, chemical
reaction . . .

(*The lights start to slowly fade. Bright, lively
'intro' music starts. The lights continue to fade
until there is just a single spot on stage. After a
few moments, he makes his entrance into the
spotlight. He is wearing the jacket, and is
obviously now in the theatre. His entrance is very
grandiose, and he does some 'over-the-top
comedy-leg' type dancing to the music. After a
few moments, the music starts to fade as he
finishes his dance.*)

Good evening!

(*The music fades out as he starts his act.*)

Very nice to be here this evening – well, at my age
it's very nice to be anywhere. Don't like getting
old – things don't work as well as they used to, do
they?

I was in the doctor's waiting room not long back,
and I overheard these three old boys talking about
their health problems.

The 70-year-old said, "My problem is I wake up every morning at seven and it takes me at least twenty minutes to pee."

The 80-year-old said, "My problem is I get up at eight and it takes me at least half an hour to have a bowel movement."

The 90-year-old said, "At seven I pee like a horse, and at eight I crap like a cow."

"So what's your problem?" asked the others.

"I don't wake up till nine!"

Don't like doctors, do you? Think they're bloody God they do. I heard about this middle-aged man who was told by his doctor that he only had twenty-four hours to live. He went home in a state of shock and fell into his wife's arms. "I've been told I've only got twenty-four hours to live," he said. "Can we have sex one last time?"

"Of course," she said, and they went to bed.

Four hours later, he turned to her and said; "Could we have sex again? I've only got twenty hours to live. It will probably be our last chance."

"Of course," she said, and they went to bed.

Eight hours later, he asked her. "Do you think we could have sex one more time? After all, I've only got twelve hours to live."

"Oh all right," she said, and they went to bed.

Four hours later, he nudged her in bed. "I just realised I've only got eight hours to live. Could we have sex one last time?"

"Very well," she sighed. "It's the least I can do in the circumstances."

Four hours later, he woke her again. "I've only got four hours to live. Would you mind if we had sex just one more time, our final act of love?"

This was too much for the wife. "Now listen," she snapped, "you may not have to get up in the morning, but I do!"

Yes . . . it's very nice to be here.

Of course I am working at a grave disadvantage tonight – I'm sober! Mind you, the last time I got really pissed wasn't good. Wasn't good at all. I'd had a terrible row with the wife, I stormed out of the house, and went and got totally pissed. I got back home very late, and because I was feeling a bit guilty, I was hoping I could make it up with her. It had all been my fault, and I wanted to say sorry.

As I say, it was very late by the time I got back, and she was in bed asleep. I crept into the bedroom, slid into the bed . . . and for the next hour I had mad passionate sex with her. Finally exhausted, I crept out to the bathroom . . . and to my horror, there was my wife lying in the bath with a mudpack on her face.

"How the hell did you get in here so quickly?" "Sssh!" she said. "You'll wake my mother."

Nightmare. Almost as bad as one of my earliest sexual experiences. I was on a date with this girl, and at the end of the evening, in the back of my car, we had sex. I wasn't very experienced, it was a bit difficult, and it was over in a matter of seconds.

Feeling quite proud of myself, I said, "If I'd known you were a virgin I'd have taken more time."

"If I'd known you were going to be that quick," she said, "I'd have taken my tights off!"

Talking of being pissed, I remember being in a bar, and towards closing time, this old man just fell off his bar-stool and couldn't get back up.

I watched him struggling to get to his feet, and decided to help him, and offered to drive him home. He was in such a bad way that he had to be dragged into the car. He wasn't happy about it, but I told him it was for the best. When we got to his house, I realised he couldn't even walk up the drive, so I carried him to the door, and rang the bell. His wife answered the door.

"I've had to bring your husband home from the bar," I explained, "because I'm afraid he's just not capable of standing, let alone walking."

"I understand," said the wife. "But tell me . . . where's his wheelchair?"

I was just trying to be friendly.

Talking of friends, this friend of mine . . . well, he used to be a friend . . . called round to see me. I wasn't in, my wife told him I wouldn't be long, and did he want to come in and wait for me. He said he would.

My wife had just had a bath, so she was in her dressing-gown. After a few moments he said to her, "I've always thought you have the most fantastic breasts. I'll pay you a hundred pounds just to see one." My wife was a bit taken aback, but thought for that sort of money, it was worth it. So she opened her robe a little and let him see one of her breasts. He gave her the hundred and then said, "I'll give you another hundred pounds if I could see the other one." So she opened her robe wider, and this time she let him have a really long look for his money. Then he gave her the hundred, got up and said, "I'm sorry, I can't wait any longer, I've got to go. Tell him I called."

When I got back, the wife said, "Your friend Mark came round earlier."

"Oh yes." I said. "Did he drop off the two hundred pounds he owes me?"

A friend of mine had his credit card stolen. He didn't report it – the thief was spending less than his wife did.

Another friend of mine went to prison. Awful it was. He was introduced to his new cellmate. "I'll take you through the week," said the cellmate.

"Sundays we go to church. Do you like church?"
"No, not much."
"Mondays we play cards. Do you like cards?"
"No, not much."
"Tuesdays we play football. Do you like football?"
"No, not much."
"Wednesdays we play snooker. Do you like snooker?"
"No, not much."
"You're hard to please, aren't you? Do you like sex?"
"Yes."
"With men or women?"
"Women."
"So you don't like sex with men?"
"No."
"Then you're not going to like Thursdays either."

Another friend of mine died recently. Minutes before the funeral, his widow took one last look in the coffin at his body. To her horror, she saw that he was wearing a brown suit whereas she had issued strict instructions to the undertaker that she wanted him buried in his blue suit, his favourite suit. She sought out the undertaker and demanded that the suit be changed.

At first, he tried to tell her that it was too late, but when he could see that she wasn't going to back down, he ordered the mortician to wheel the trolley away.

A few minutes later, just as the funeral was about to start, the coffin was wheeled back in, and incredibly, the corpse was now wearing a blue suit. The widow was delighted and, after the service, praised the undertaker for his swift work.

"Oh it was nothing," he said. "It so happened there was another body in the back room and he was already dressed in a blue suit. All we had to do was switch the heads!"

Thank you very much, you've been a lovely audience, and I'll see you again soon.

Goodnight!

(*The spotlight fades as he leaves the stage. End of Act One.*)

## ACT TWO

THE MAN *enters, crosses and sits in front of the mirror.*

My God, you did it!  You did it!

(*He turns to the audience.*)

I did it!

(*He takes off his jacket, gets a couple of tissues, and mops his face.*)

It was so hot out there.  I'd no idea those lights would be so hot.  Shouldn't have bothered with the jacket.

(*He gets up and moves around, still 'hyped'.*)

I feel so . . . so . . . actually I'm not sure how I feel. I'm still shaking.  Got through it all right though. Can't say I actually enjoyed it, I was too busy thinking about what comes next.  I completely forgot where I was at one point.

And I can't believe I forgot the furniture salesman joke.  Can you believe that?  I was going to start with that one.  I got too carried away with the dancing, that was the trouble, and I just froze . . . right at the start.  Can't remember what I said . . . oh yes, something about getting older.  Actually, maybe that's more appropriate.  After what I've just done I feel I've aged ten years!

God, what an experience.  Some of the stuff went really well.  Some didn't . . . but it doesn't matter. I've done it!  I've done it!

A drink, that's what I need, a drink.  I've got one stashed away here somewhere.

(*He crosses and gets a little tin out of one of the drawers in the chest of drawers. He takes it out carefully and pours some of the contents into a tin cup. He approaches the audience and raises the cup.*)

Cheers.

(*He takes a swig.*)

Aah . . . that's hit the spot. God, I can't remember when I last felt like this. This . . . 'buzz'. I mean, you don't get this very often do you?

(*He takes another swig.*)

Parachute jumping, that might do it . . . well it would for me. I couldn't do it, could you?  Anyone here jumped out of a plane?

(*He looks for a response.*)

Must be mad.

I suppose some people would think it mad what I've just done. Takes all sorts I suppose.

I wonder if Billy Connolly felt like this after his debut?  Or Jackie Mason? Of course they all started younger than me. Easier when you're young, you don't care do you? No responsibilities, no worries . . . all you've got to think about is where your next sexual experience is coming from.  When will you next get to visit the inner thigh?

(*He takes another swig of the drink.*)

I still can't believe I did it.  Over thirty years I've waited.  Thirty years.

(*He stops.*)

One of the blokes backstage said I did really well.
And he does all the shows. Mind you, it helped
that I was following that idiot ventriloquist. I mean
. . . if you're not very good at something, why do
it? His lips were moving all over the place. Even I
could do better than that.

(*He says the following without moving his lips.*)

"Hello all . . . Derek the Donkey here."

How about that? Told you I could it better than
him. Poor sod. I'd hate to get booed, wouldn't
you? Because that's not an easy audience out
there, that lot.

(*He finishes off the drink and takes the cup back
to the table.*)

I suppose I ought to get this make-up off.

(*He looks in the mirror.*)

I might do it differently next time . . . the bloke
backstage said I looked like a poof. I don't think I
did, do you? (*He looks at the audience.*)  Do you?
Actually, don't answer that, I'd rather not know.

(*He starts taking the make-up off using some
removal cream, and then wiping it off with
tissues.*)

One of the other blokes in the show lent me this
cream. He seems very 'au-fait' with make-up that
one . . . I'd say that he very definitely glides to the
other end of the ballroom.

(*A moment.*)

I still can't believe I've done it you know.  After
thirty years.

(*He continues removing the make-up throughout
the following, using tissues and then the towel. At

*various points he stops when he wants to focus
directly on the audience.*)

Not that easy to get rid of this stuff is it? No
wonder you girls spend so much time in front of
the mirror. Mind you, the lads are just as bad
these days aren't they? Have you seen all those
products on the market for men? Moisturisers,
hair-gel, shower-gel, underarm deodorant,
underbum deodorant . . . they've got everything.

Glad they didn't have those things in my day, this
is too much like hard work. And waxing! All this
bloody waxing they do. Back, crack and sack.

(*He gets up and mimes dancing at the disco, then
meeting someone.*) Oh yes, I've had the sack done
. . . look . . . (*He mimes pulling down the front of
his trousers.*) . . . and the crack . . . (*He then mimes
exposing his bum.*) God, can you imagine?

(*A moment.*)

So where was I . . . before we were so rudely
interrupted?

Oh yes . . . the house . . . I was telling you about
the house. Judith got an offer on the house.

So . . . she was jumping for joy, and I was walking
about in a catatonic state. Okay I thought, it's not
the end of the world. Maybe it's not the right
time. And as I always say . . . what's the worst
that could happen?

Well, nothing really. I don't have to lose my
dream . . . just postpone it for a while. Later on I
could be a comedian in Oxford or Bath, or
wherever we end up. Why not? They need their
laughter too.

(*He sits back down and continues taking off his
make-up. As before, he keeps stopping
throughout as he addresses the audience.*)

I was beginning to accept it, that my life was
about to change for the worse . . . that I would be
leaving the city, breeding dogs in the country . . .
when the phone call came.  Right out of the blue.
Talk about timing.

It was one of the comedy club owners I'd been to
see.

"I've got this bloke coming to the club, looking for
new talent." He said. "I thought of you, so if you
don't mind doing your act in front of two people,
they'll give you an audition."

"No, I don't mind."
"They won't laugh of course."
"That's all right."
"Okay, next Tuesday at 11.30."
"I'll be there."

I was so excited I was almost jumping up and
down. Then Judith yells from the kitchen. "Who
was that?"

Right . . . gird the loins, here we go.

"That was er, that was one of the club-owners.
They've offered me an audition."
"No! We have a deal."
"It's a wonderful opportunity."
"No!"
"It's very unusual for this to happen."
"No!!"
"I might not even get the job."
"No!! We have a deal!!
"I can't not go."
"No, no, no, no, no, no, no, no, no!!"

"So you don't want me to go is that it?"

What a row we had.

Now at this point, I have to tell you, we have
never actually had food flying around our house
. . . we've never had that sort of row before.

That level was now reached.

I don't know if any of you blokes here have had
food thrown at you, but it's not fun is it?

Oh it may look fun in the films, but in real life . . .

(*He rises.*)

You see what one forgets is, that not only is it
flying around and dangerous, but also . . . it is
bloody hot!

Boiling hot spaghetti coiled round the forearm is
not a very pleasant experience I can assure you.

I had hot Bolognaise sauce all over my shirt, it
wasn't pretty, and certainly wasn't comfortable.
Obviously I got out of there as quickly as I could.

So the next few days were not very
communicative.

I sulked around, pretending I wasn't going for the
job . . . but obviously I was going for it. I had to
didn't I? Couldn't turn down an opportunity like
that.

I rehearsed secretly, in earnest . . . either in quiet
moments at work, or when I was walking in the
park. Not easy that, with people thinking I was
the obligatory loony. Little old ladies would give
me a wide berth and a steely glare.

(*He sits again and continues taking off his make-
up.*)

Meanwhile, new house details were pouring in, all
these 'suitable for dog-breeding' type houses in

the countryside . . . and I could see Judith getting
more and more excited.

I treated the whole thing with total disinterest . . .
so she used to share the excitement with her
sister, Sarah. I'd be sitting in the other room and
could hear their animated chattering.

"This one's got two bathrooms . . . oh, I love the
kitchen in this one . . . oooh, look at that garden"
. . . you know the sort of thing.

So there I was . . . sitting on my own, and thinking
. . . pity really, because I wanted to be in there
with Sarah.

I know, I know . . . I was supposed to forget about
what happened all those years ago . . . but I
couldn't. I just loved looking at her.

She still never gave anything away. She behaved
as if she really had forgotten all about it. Always
very friendly with me, always talkative, but no
more. Not a hint of anything. Maybe she really
had forgotten, maybe it wasn't just an act.

(*He has now finished taking off his make-up.*)

But one day . . . a week or so later . . . something
happened. After all those years . . . something
happened.

(*He rises.*)

No, no . . . it's not what you're thinking . . . it was
a look. That's right . . . a look. It lasted about five
seconds.

Now that might not sound much to you, but it was
monumental to me.

She and Roger had been round for supper, and
they were just leaving. Roger and Judith were in
the front garden, saying goodnight on the path,

and we were in the hall about to go out and join
them. We stopped to say goodnight, and our eyes
met.

Now, our eyes had met many times before, in many
similar situations . . . but this time it was different.
I don't know why, I don't know what was going
on in her life . . . her inner life . . . but for whatever
reason, this was different.

It was like the whole world just . . . stopped. Our
eyes were locked together. Whatever feelings
were deep inside me, and whatever feelings were
deep inside her . . . 'connected' at that moment.
We both . . . 'knew'.

Five seconds, that's all it was. I would never have
believed it, but you can really feel a lot in five
seconds . . . if it's 'real'. Amazing.

(*He stops and looks at them.*)

You ought to try it sometime . . . with someone.
Don't say anything, it has to be silent. It's just a
look, deep into their eyes, and don't look away.
For five seconds. That's longer than you'd
normally look isn't it? Now if that person you
were looking at was trying to tell you something
through their eyes, I bet you'd feel something.
Well . . . I know you would. You try it and see.

Anyway, the point is, I certainly felt something . . .
I was quite shocked. She must have always known
how I felt, I was always thinking things as I looked
at her . . . but as I say, she never, ever gave
anything away. Until that moment. And I knew. I
knew she still had feelings for me. I knew it. But
before I could say anything, she broke the moment
and hurried out to join the others. And never
referred to it again. Pretended again that nothing
had happened.

But I 'knew'.

Actually, there was a film with a moment like that.
Oh I know everyone always talks about
*Casablanca*, the look between Humphrey Bogart
and Ingrid Bergman . . . but the film I'm talking
about is called *Heaven Can Wait* with Warren
Beatty and Julie Christie.

What a beautiful couple they were. Ever see that
film? There's a moment near the end of the film
where they meet in a tunnel. He's in another body,
so she doesn't know who he is, and he doesn't
know who she is. But their 'souls' know who they
really are, and they know that they really love
each other. The moment when their eyes meet,
quizzical, strange, and yet 'knowing' . . . is,
without doubt, one of the finest filmic moments I
think I've ever seen. I don't know how they did it.
It's worth seeing the film for that moment alone.
It'll make you tingle. And we all like a bit of
tingling now and again don't we?

I bet Roger never makes her tingle. God, what a
pillock he is.

(*He stops.*)

Interesting though isn't it . . . all these things?

I'll tell you what else is interesting. While we're
on the subject of silent moments . . . well, it was
interesting to me anyway. A while ago, I was
passing a war memorial and there was a group of
people doing a one-minute silence. I didn't even
know it was the anniversary of anything . . .
terrible thing to admit I know, but I stood with
them anyway.

And I thought of something that I'd read
somewhere.

I know I should have been thinking about the
'fallen heroes', but you know how minds work
sometimes, and I remember reading that the French
philosopher, Blaise Pascal, said that – and I'm not

sure I'm quoting his exact words here – he said
that 'most of humankind's problems were the
result of their not being able to cope with silence'.

And I thought that quite interesting. Because it's
never silent is it?

And it seems even worse now. Kids are watching
television, playing a computer game, and listening
to music all at the same time. I think Blaise was
right . . . we can't cope with silence.

As I was standing there, at the war memorial, I
thought . . . I never do this. I'm hardly ever in
silence. I have music at home and in the car, I
have TV, I seek people to talk to . . . I'm hardly
ever in silence. And I'm sure it's the same for you.
And if we're not used to silence, how can we learn
to cope with it.

(*He stops and looks at the audience.*)

I'll tell you what we'll do. We'll have a one-
minute silence . . . right now. Okay? Let's do it.
Please. Indulge me. I'll time us. Let's see how we
cope.

(*He looks at his watch.*)

Okay, ready? One-minute silence . . . now.

(*He then gives a one-minute silence. He keeps
checking his watch throughout the minute, and
just looks at the audience.*)

Okay, time's up. Mmmm, interesting, wouldn't
you say? I'd love to know what was going on in
your heads. On second thoughts, maybe it's best
that I don't know.

(*A moment.*)

Anyway . . . where was I? What was I saying?

Oh yes . . . they were going through the house details, and I was gearing myself up for the audition at the comedy club.

Tuesday came, and I woke up shaking. The old chemical reaction again. I left the house as usual, changed at work into a suitable costume – not quite as outrageous as this – and then shot round to the club.

I knocked at the door.
"Yeah?"
"I've come for the audition."
"You've come for the what?"
"The audition."
"Audition? You were supposed to be here yesterday."
"Yesterday? You told me Tuesday."
"I phoned you and left a message. They changed the day."
"Message? I didn't get any message."
"Well I left one. I spoke to your wife myself."
"My wife? But I never got the message."
"Sorry mate, nothing I can do now."
"But I must have the audition."
"Sorry, but you've blown it."
"Can't I audition for you?"
"I can't make it any plainer . . . now sod off!"

And with that, he slammed the door in my face.

I didn't go back to work, I went straight home. Judith was sitting at the kitchen table having coffee with old Mrs Jones from next-door.

"You're home early." she says sweetly.
"Why didn't you give me that message?" I say sweetly.
"What message is that?" she says sweetly.
"You know what f–ing message!" I say. Not so sweetly this time.
"Let's not row in front of Mrs Jones." she says.
"You're right, you're quite right." I turned to Mrs Jones. "You. Out!"

She was off like a shot. I've never seen her move
so fast.

Now, I don't lose my temper very often, but when
I do . . .

I went mad. I wanted to hit her. But I don't hit
women as you know . . . because of my mother . . .
so I hit everything else instead. The door, the
fridge, the table, the wall . . . I threw a chair I think
. . . and then I ripped up all the house details,
yelling, "We're not moving, we're not f–ing
moving! Do you hear me?"

She was really frightened. She'd never seen me
like that before. She tried to calm me down.

"Just calm down for God's sake."

"Don't f–ing try to calm me down, I haven't
finished being angry yet!"

I picked up a china figurine. It was her favourite
piece. Quite valuable too.

"Don't you dare!" she yelled.
"Don't you dare dare me!" I yelled back.

She rushed over to grab it from me . . . and I hurled
it to the floor. It smashed into pieces . . . and she
started smashing into me. I pushed her away,
stormed out of the house, and slammed the door.

God I was angry.

And you know what I really hate when I'm angry?
Someone saying to me really sweetly, "Don't be
angry." God that makes me angry.
I mean, what are you supposed to do? Stop being
angry right there and then? Anger doesn't work
like that. It doesn't just stop. Can you imagine?

(*angrily*) "I'm angry!"
(*sweetly*) "Don't be angry."

(*sweetly*)  "Oh all right then."

Of course it doesn't work like that.  Anger doesn't
just stop . . . it subsides . . . over time.

She shouldn't have told me to calm down.

(*A moment.*)

Anyway, I was almost in tears as I stormed down
the street. I didn't know where I was going. I
turned the corner, and almost bumped into Sarah.
She was just nipping round to see Judith. She
could see what a state I was in, so she persuaded
me to go to her house.

I explained what had happened, she told me to
wait there . . . and went round to check on Judith.
She was obviously a bit worried, because as I said
before, Judith's never been a very healthy
individual. Very 'frail' she is.

Anyway, to cut a long story short, it turned out to
be a nightmare. Sarah arrived to find Judith
slumped on the floor.  She'd had a stroke. They
had to rush her to hospital. What a nightmare.

(*He stops for a moment.*)

The stroke turned out to be a massive one.  She
ended up almost totally paralysed.

God, can you imagine?  She couldn't walk, she
couldn't feed herself, couldn't talk . . . she
couldn't do anything.

A nightmare.

(*He stops again.*)

We had a carer who came in to help out, but most
of the time it was down to me.

(*He moves across, picks up the chair and carries it across to the bed.*)

I fed her, changed her, lifted her, tried to keep her comfortable, read to her, gave her the pain-killers, massaged her, washed her . . . I did everything. And can you imagine the guilt I felt?

Months it went on . . . and she never got any better.

(*He moves round, positions the chair at the side of the bed and sits.*)

She was obviously in a lot of pain all the time, and we had this little thing when I gave her the pain-killers.

She couldn't talk properly . . . she just made little grunting noises . . . and when I gave her a pain-killer, if the pain was really bad that day she'd grunt for another one. One day she tried to get me to give her four pills . . . must have been bad. I didn't of course, but it was difficult to see the pain in her eyes.

I just prayed that she would fall asleep.

Sarah obviously came round a lot, and that was a real help. We used to sit either side of Judith's bed, talking across her.

(*He indicates that Sarah is sitting on the other side of the bed.*)

Judith would be drifting in and out of sleep as we carried on talking and sharing the 'chores'. I don't know what I'd have done if she hadn't been there. I think I'd have gone mad.

She was obviously very concerned for her sister . . . but she never lost her sense of humour. She knew Judith was always physically 'weak', it had driven her mad when they were kids so she was

used to being 'supportive'. But I knew it was hard
for her.  She said I was a real help to her.

Sometimes we'd be talking, and then suddenly
we'd realise that Judith was fast asleep. Time just
passed so quickly when we were together. We'd
then make sure Judith was all right, tuck her in
properly, that sort of thing . . . and then move
downstairs and carry on talking.

(*He rises and moves across to centre.*)

Quite often she didn't seem in any hurry to get
home. "Why should I rush back?" she said,
"Roger's always so bloody miserable."

As you know, I've always thought that. He's a
boring, miserable pillock is Roger.  I told you, I
don't understand why she ever married him. He's
always so negative. You hear about some people
who always think the glass if half-full, and others
who think the glass is half-empty.  Roger has
trouble finding the glass!  That's how bad he is.

I said to him the other week, "Your hollyhocks
look nice."

"They've got blackfly!" he replied.

So you try again. "These roses are a beautiful
colour."

"They were supposed to be pink!"

In the end you think, 'well sod you then', and you
stop talking. But I'd never heard her say it before,
that he was so 'bloody miserable' . . . she's always
so protective of him.

"Oh I'm sure you could cheer him up," I said,
"with that smile of yours."

(*He stops.*)

Yes, I know, that is such a 'cheesy' line, but I meant it. She has the most wonderful smile. It lights up her face . . . in fact, I think it lights up the whole room.

"Oh no," she said, "there's no smiling in our house."

"But you seem to smile all the time."

She looked at me. "I do when I'm with you."

(*He stops.*)

Amazing isn't it? The power of words. Six and a half words, that's all it was.

(*He counts the words on his fingers as he says the line.*)

"I do when I'm with you."

Amazing how something so seemingly small could be, well . . . life-changing.

People often say that don't they? "It changed my life." "Bumped into so and so, went into this shop . . . decided to do this instead of that . . ."

Small things can be so . . . huge.

I remember a friend of mine was taking a flight, to Rome I think it was . . . he got to the airport, and for some reason he didn't want to get on the plane. The friend that was with him thought he was just being stupid . . . 'It's the safest form of transport . . . everyone gets nervous flying . . . don't be so ridiculous . . .'

But whatever his friend tried, my friend would not get onto that plane. Walked out of the airport instead.

And can you guess what happened?

That's right.  As he walked out of the airport, he bumped into an old 'flame' of his that he hadn't seen for years and they're now married with two wonderful children.

Isn't that amazing?

(*He stops and looks at the audience.*)

What?  What did you think was going to happen?

Anyway . . . when she said that to me, it was like a small electric shock going right through me. She'd always hidden what she may or may not have felt about me, you know, after what happened all those years ago . . . but it just came out . . . "I do when I'm with you." Only six and a half words, but they meant so much.

She could see the effect it had on me . . . I walked over to hold her, she stopped me. "I have to go. I'm sorry." She couldn't look at me, and just hurried out of the house.

(*He moves back up to the chair and sits at the side of the bed.*)

She didn't come back for a couple of days, and when she did, she once again tried to pretend that nothing had happened. We just sat either side of Judith's bed, chatting away . . . and when we moved downstairs she just excused herself and went home.

Until one night.

She'd obviously had a row with Roger before she came round . . . she was really upset, and anyway, to cut a long story short, she'd actually been defending me. Apparently Roger totally blamed me for what's happened to Judith.

I also blame me.  Of course I do.

And in fact it was Sarah that helped me deal with the guilt. She said it was quite normal for married couples to have rows now and then, but that Judith's condition was not normal . . . never has been. She didn't have a stroke when we'd rowed before – of course it didn't help that it was a big row – but no one could have anticipated that this would happen.

Anyway, Roger was being his usual negative, boring and miserable self, and she found herself defending me, and because she defended me so strongly, the whole thing got totally out of hand and all sorts of things were said.

She was clearly very upset, and I reached across the bed and took her hand.

She didn't pull away.

We must have been holding hands for about ten seconds – and that is a long time under the circumstances – before we glanced round at Judith.

She was asleep.

We continued to hold hands as she then started to talk . . . and it all came out.

About how terrible life has been for her with Roger. About how different he was from the man she married. About how his constant negativity was getting her down. About how little she smiled in her own house. On and on she went . . . until finally, she broke down.

Judith was still asleep.

(*He rises and moves around to the other side of the bed.*)

I slowly got up and went round to the other side
of the bed, and took her in my arms. She didn't
resist, and didn't try to pull away.

We stood there a while, holding onto each other,
and then I gently led her downstairs.

(*He moves away from the bed.*)

At the bottom of the stairs I stopped, took her
face in my hands . . . and gently kissed her. She
didn't resist, and didn't try to pull away.

We went into the living-room . . .

(*A moment.*)

I think you can use your imagination for the next
bit.

(*He stops.*)

You probably think that was terrible of me . . . with
my wife upstairs . . . but we thought it terrible too.

But we couldn't stop. And we did try. Quite a
few times.

(*He stops.*)

It became like a routine. She'd come round . . .
help with Judith . . . talk across Judith until she
was fully asleep . . . and then downstairs.

Oh God . . . I love her so much.

(*He stops again.*)

It was wonderful. For both of us. It was 'two-
way'. I've never known anything like it. I should
have married her in the first place.

We couldn't keep our hands off each other. It was almost 'unreal'. It was like a total 'emotional release'.

A release for her from the years of a terrible, almost loveless marriage . . . a release for me from the 'controlling' inhibition of my marriage . . . a regular and momentary release from her guilt . . . a regular and momentary release from my guilt . . . a release of her deep-felt feelings for me . . . and a release of my deep-felt feelings for her. I know this all sounds like excuses for our behaviour . . . but that's how it was.

During all this Judith never seemed to get any better, if anything she was getting slightly worse.

Weeks and weeks this went on . . . and then one night it stopped!

Sarah couldn't bear the guilt any more . . . and it just stopped. She still came round but it was very business-like. She helped with Judith, talked to her, no holding hands with me, just . . . 'business-like'.

I couldn't bear it. And no matter how hard I tried to get her to talk, no matter that I could still see the love in her eyes, she wouldn't budge. Her mind was made up.

We had a terrible row one night. I wouldn't let her out of the door – I was desperate – but she wouldn't give in . . . we were trying to keep our voices down . . . and finally she pushed me aside and left.

I was distraught.

I had a couple of drinks . . . or maybe more . . . and then I went up to check on Judith.

(*He moves across, and again sits at the side of the bed.*)

She was awake.

She couldn't speak, but there was this look in her
eye. Maybe I just 'imagined' it, maybe it was my
guilt, maybe she'd heard us . . . I don't know what
it was. But there was 'something'.

I tried to distract the situation and asked her if she
was in pain. She nodded. I gave her a pain-killer.

She grunted for another one. I gave her another
one. She grunted again. I looked at her. She held
my gaze, and grunted again. I hesitated a moment,
she grunted again . . . and I gave her another one.
She grunted again. I said, no.

Then she made this . . . 'noise'. It was almost
frightening in its intensity.

She continued to stare at me, almost right through
me . . . as though she 'knew'.

I was shocked.

She made the noise again. I could see that she was
struggling, but couldn't move. There was a
desperation in her eyes. She made the noise again
. . . this time louder. I gave her another one . . .
again the noise . . . again the noise!

I gave her another one . . . again the noise. I didn't
say anything . . . again the noise! I looked at her,
and this time the noise was different. Quieter . . .
almost pleading. There were tears in her eyes.

Again the quiet noise.

We both 'knew'.

I gave her another one, again the noise . . .
another one . . . the noise . . . another one . . . the
noise . . . another one . . . the noise . . .

The whole bottle.

I stayed just looking at her for ages. She looked at me vacantly for a while . . . and then her gaze altered, and she focused on another part of the room.

(*He rises and moves around, a little way from the bed.*)

Eventually I got up and went downstairs, and had another drink. I was very calm I seem to remember. It was all very quiet. I went back to look at her after about half an hour . . . and she was sleeping. She looked so peaceful . . .

I didn't go back until the next morning.

(*He moves in and sits on the side of the bed. He then slowly pulls the sheet up and covers the pillow. He then starts to break down quietly. After awhile he tries to pull himself together.*)

I'm sorry . . . I'm sorry . . .

(*He rises, goes over to the chest of drawers and starts to take off his costume. He picks up the folded clothes and puts them on – it is a blue shirt and dark blue trousers, obviously prisoner's clothing.*)

Thirty years I've waited to make my debut. The prison officer who organised the concert was very pleased. Immediately after the show he booked me for the Christmas show. So that's good . . . thing's are looking up.

Six years I've been here now . . . and yes, thing's are looking up.

(*A moment.*)

I don't remember much about the court case. Because there was a court case.

The day-carer had reported that a new bottle of
pills had been used up. They found an excess of
the drug inside her . . . I can't remember all the
medical evidence, that courtroom's a blur. I don't
even remember my cross-examination.

I remember Sarah's though. She was so upset and
angry. You see, she was convinced I'd killed
Judith because of the row we'd had when she
stopped the affair. But it wasn't just an 'affair', it
was more than that. I truly loved her. She
assumed I'd killed Judith, and made it look like an
accident, so that she and I could then be together.

Anyway, in the courtroom, she kept calling me a
murderer, and what a bastard I was, it was like a
nightmare. To hear that from the woman I love.

And to prove to the court that I had a motive for
murder, she confessed to the affair. Everyone was
shocked when they heard this I seem to remember.
Making love downstairs, your dying sister
upstairs . . . she didn't get a lot of sympathy. My
lawyer made it even worse for her . . . I've never
seen such a character-assassination. She just
broke down . . . it was awful. I felt so sorry for her.

He then talked about 'mercy-killing'. About how
there was no medical evidence to suggest that
Judith would ever get better, about the pressure I
was under seeing my beloved wife suffering so
much . . . about how I'd been punished enough.

An 'act of mercy', he called it, an act of 'kindness'
from a broken man who couldn't bear what was
happening to his wife. There was doubt in the
jury's mind.

Not guilty!

(*He stops, goes across to the table and pours the
rest of the drink into the cup.*)

I'd been in custody for about four months before the trial started . . . and after I was found not guilty, it was really strange going home.

Oh I didn't care what the neighbours thought, I was going to move away from there as soon as I could anyway . . . but I did care about Sarah. And I knew I'd never see her again . . . well, not in the way that I wanted to see her.

Not after that court case.

And I kept thinking about the verdict. Not guilty.

I agreed with what the lawyer said, it was terrible to see Judith like that . . . it was terrible to know that she would never get better . . . to know that we were all waiting for her to die . . . to see the pain she was in. And there was a sort of 'kindness' to what I did. It was an 'act of mercy'.

(*He finishes the drink, and puts the cup back on the table.*)

But I couldn't stop thinking about what Sarah had said either. Was there a part of me, when I was giving Judith the pills . . . was there a part of me thinking, 'this could turn out for the best'? I don't mean consciously. Consciously I was involved with Judith and that moment. But subconsciously, who knows what goes on in there? Maybe I did think this was an opportunity for Sarah and me.

And while I was thinking all this, there was a knock at the front door.

It was Roger. And he was angry. Very angry.

First time I'd seen him so animated. He started pushing me, calling me a murderer. Told me what a bastard I was. How could I have done it . . . to my wife's sister . . . and how dare I touch his wife!

He started punching out . . . I was desperately trying to defend myself, he was kicking and punching and yelling, I backed into the living room, and he caught me with a punch. I fell over by the fireplace, I grabbed the poker and threatened him with it . . . he just kept coming . . . I made a few wild swings, just to keep him at a distance, I tried to get to the door, I was still swinging, I was nearly there . . . he walked right into one of the swings, and fell to the ground.

I should have just run away there and then . . . but I didn't.

I just swung again, and again, and again . . . and again.

(*He stops.*)

Manslaughter they said, not murder.

They say everyone's capable of murder you know. It's in all of us. But most people don't, do they?

I've had a lot of time to think about it, and all I keep coming up with is . . . how the hell did it happen? I just wanted to be a stand-up comedian, that's all. I didn't want this.

(*A moment.*)

Anyway, at least my goals are clear now. There's new material to get together for the Christmas show, and then I'll have to start thinking about next year's concert. Be good practice for when I get out. Shouldn't be too long . . . if I behave myself. And if I keep making them laugh, that should help.

And I'll make them laugh all right . . . oh yes . . . I'll make the bastard's laugh. I'll try and find some more prison jokes, they went very well.

(*He crosses back up and sits at the table.*)

And I'll remember to put that furniture salesman joke in next time.

(*He looks in the mirror.*)

Before I became a stand-up comedian . . .

(*The lights start to fade.*)

. . . I used to be a furniture salesman . . .

(*The lights fade. The end.*)